What Happens

THE GALILEO PRESS LTD.

Baltimore, Maryland

What Happens

ROBERT LONG

Published by The Galileo Press, Ltd.,
15201 Wheeler Lane, Sparks, Maryland 21152.
Production by Kachergis Book Design, Pittsboro, North Carolina.
Cover Painting: "Hot Sheets (Anxiety)" by Josh Dayton.
Publication of this book was made possible in part
by a grant from the Maryland State Arts Council.

LIBRARY OF CONGRESS CATALOGING-IN-PUBLICATION DATA

Long, Robert, 1954–
What happens / Robert Long. — 1st ed.
p.   cm.
ISBN 0-913123-19-6 (pbk.) : $9.95 (est.)
I. Title. PS3562.O4947W5   1988
811'.54—dc 19   88-9423 CIP

FIRST EDITION

Acknowledgments

Some of these poems first appeared in the following periodicals
and anthologies:

The American Scholar: December

Anthology of Magazine Verse (1981, 1984, 1985 editions): Water,
Burning Out, Chelsea, What Happens

Aspen Anthology: What's So Funny 'Bout Peace, Love and Under-
standing

Bridgehampton Sun: Old Story, Poem, Saying One Thing, What It Is

City Paper (Baltimore): East Ninth Street, Littoral Landscape

Crazyhorse: East Ninth Street, Elegy for My Grandfather, Have a
Nice Day

East Hampton Star: Footnote

Fire Island Tide: Montauk Point

Indiana Review: Found and Lost, Time and Its Double

Kayak: Burning Out, Water, What Happens

Maryland Poetry Review: East Ninth Street

New American Poets of the 8os: Burning Out, Chelsea, Debts, First
Day of Spring, Somewhere on the Coast of Maine

New York Gedichte (Munich): Chelsea

The New Yorker: April Again, Chelsea, Debts, First Day of Spring,
Montauk Point

Poetry: Dreaming, Goodbye, Hot Air, Interior Decoration, In the
Unfinished House, In the Red, Old Story, Perfect Sunset, Poem,
Saying One Thing, Strange Insects, Thruway, What It Is

Scrub Oak Review: Littoral Landscape

Tendril: Cairo, Leaving Vermont

"Two Shades of Gray" was a broadside from LIU/Southampton.

"Poem" appeared in a collaboration with artist Alfonso Ossorio for
Guild Hall Museum, 1981.

A number of poems appeared in the chapbooks *Getting Out Of Town*
(1978) and *What It Is* (1981), both from Street Press.

Special thanks to Mary Karr, David Wojahn, Stephen Dobyns and
Heather McHugh for their help with the poems, and to the PEN
Writers Fund for a grant in 1986.

for my mother, in memory of my father,
and in memory of Howard Moss

I prefer "you" in the plural, I want "you,"
You must come to me, all golden and pale,
Like the dew and the air.
And then I start getting this feeling of exaltation.
—JOHN ASHBERY, "A Blessing in Disguise"

What I really loved today
was New York, its streets and
men selling flowers and hot dogs
in them. Mysterious town houses,
the gritty wind.
—JAMES SCHUYLER, "Back"

Contents

IV

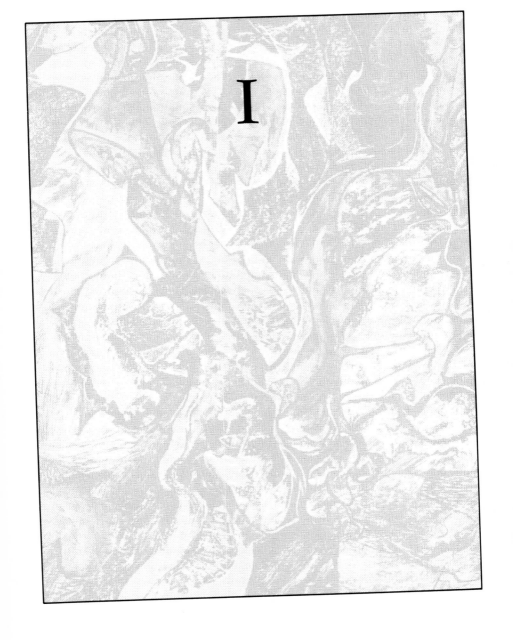

I

Water

Today was one of those days so clear
That you think you can see the future.
People walked on thin ice, on the bay.
Sunlight everywhere. When the sun went down,
Small black clouds began marching across the horizon.
All the neon in town started to hum.

Now, it's a quarter past two,
And everyone else is out dancing, or asleep,
Which is fine if you're asleep.
The heat's time bomb ticks in the walls.
Rain falls softly on the firehouse;
Water gurgles in drains.

I remember sitting at a picture window,
Watching the sun go out,
The dock lights come on.
There was something unpleasant about the scene:
The harbor moved in a little shiver,
Like an electrocardiogram.

When I was thirteen,
I had a tendency to fall off docks.
I didn't do it on purpose; it just happened.
Once, my foot got caught in a bulkhead,
And I hung underwater until someone pulled me out.
He just happened to be walking by.
There was no one else around.

Littoral Landscape

Last night, in a dream, a woman
Called on the phone to ask if I'd like to order
A case of instant rice pilaf. Today,
I'm "taking in" the September sun
On an afternoon so mirror-like and bluish
It seems Windexed. Volkswagens sputter by.
Cumulus clouds, neat shelves of periwinkle,
Slide north, over Shelter Island, Plum Gut,
Orient, in the general direction of the genteel shore
Of Connecticut, the state I know best

From the inside of a stalled Amtrak express,
On its way to or from Montreal. Here,
The glassy harbor fibrillates with shiners
Seen through drowsy cattails and clumps
Of delphinium, zinnia, phlox. I used to paint,
But it was too messy, and turpentine
Gave me a headache. By the time I got cleaned up,
It was time to go to bed. Those days,
I worked in a bakery making chocolate cigarettes,
Reported at 5 a.m. sharp. I was younger then.

Now, I'm old and crabby and don't even like the beach—
Too much sand, water too cold, noisy children,
Etc. These days I prefer to watch things happen—
An egret gliding into marsh grass, people
Falling off bicycles—from my bright green
Redwood chair. If Long Island is a lobster claw
Adjunct to the malformed lobster body
Of the Mid-Atlantic States, I'm sitting on the periphery
Of a minuscule barnacle about to close on Gardiner's Island:
Tidal waves, Stanford Whites swept crunching out to sea.

It was like that during the most recent hurricane
(Gloria, 1985): plastic boats thrashing at moorings,
Elms riven on Main Street, the one-sided
Tic-tac-toe of shop windows for fifty miles around,
Each game pointlessly complete, existentially satisfying.
Today, not much sound: the echo of far-off carpenters
Building something hideous in the pine woods, a dog
Barking at a nervous boy on a rusting Schwinn, invisible birds.
Somewhere, my cat is decapitating mice, after playing with them.
This painterly day, the willows seem palette-knifed onto the sky.

Burning Out

I shot pool in a bar last night,
With a pal. Someone was playing the piano badly:
Show tunes, mostly. The room was filled
With smoke from the fireplace, cigarettes, pot.
There was a complex curtain in the air.

I told my friend I hated to see him drinking so much,
Hanging out with self-destructive people,
Running up tabs and running out of rope.
We're old friends, since high school.
He sank the seven. I chalked up.

Lying on my stomach in bed, at seventeen,
After a tab of four-way sunshine,
I knew that all energy emanates from the solar plexus.
I'd seen the sun, a miraculous red pill,
On the wall. I loved everything; anything was special.

Once, I talked someone down from a bad trip.
He said everything was on fire; I told him he was right.
We sat there watching the rain come down.
I knew this other kid, a good athlete,
Who jumped out a window when he was twenty.

The last time I saw him, his eyes were like
Two cigarette burns. We drove around
Until we were both sick to death with the whole thing.
I told him to call me that night, after work:
We could talk. But he didn't.

This is me talking my head off,
Saying I grew up, where did you go?
This is me talking to you in a metallic voice,
Through tin cans on string, across backyards with blue wash flapping,
Saying I loved you, saying goodbye.

Montauk Point

The magic starts
where the road unwinds into space
like the final dive from a barstool
and the lighthouse throws its arms
past the quiet confetti of mainland.

What looks good in headlights
turns to dust under the sun.
Almost home, the car swallows the stripe.

The dipper handle points
to the end of land, where car lights fade
into spirit light,
a mass of wet granules that drop
mote-like to the sea:
black, gray, white.

Poem

Someone you loved is dead,
So you go about things
As if you were dead, too. Definition:
Careful gardening,
Highly polished shoes,
Lots of smiles and nods
And affable conversation.

After a few years of this,
You notice one day a carton
Of mildewed espadrilles in the basement,
Black flowers in the yard, and,
Running out of a bush,
A small child, singing to himself,
With a broken truck in his hands.

Thruway

Say the highway left us over there:
Insects humming, a boy in a kayak
Paddling aimlessly from one side of a pond
To the other, then back again.

If you can believe the maps,
There's a way out from under these clouds,
Clouds like slowly exploding brain matter.
It'll be like opening a door

On unexpected snow, or the way you felt
Right after your first haircut. But right now
We'll just stay in this car,
Maintain a low profile. Next week,

Things might seem different, seem themselves
Brought to a higher power, like that billboard
With the giant cigarette on it, receding now
In the rear-view mirror.

Cairo

Because you're there,
I think about this city, day leading into night
As inexorably as *a* is followed by *b*.
Everywhere, I feel the atoms of you

Reassembling, disassembling
Like the shifting clouds, the forsythia
That's here today, gone tomorrow.
This is the virtue of time-lapse photography.

And I can see the blizzards coming.
Leaves, stiff and crisp, skate on asphalt.
The cat stalks a cricket
On the damp green rug. The sky's gray.

It's as if your absence
Were more real
Than if you were here, right now.
This is the beginning

Of the end of the world,
Its motion inhibited by starts of fear:
Pyramids collapsing into yellow dust.
Each morning, we get up the same way:

Stunned, disconsolate.

Have a Nice Day

"We live in an age of hyenas." —REUBEN NAKIAN

The romance of police in their shiny cruisers washes
Across television screens as well as everyone's windows,
Here in New York, through the first-floor triple-locked
Kind as well as the big, barroom plate-glass type,
Street level, blurred with transient figures: going to work,

Going home, etc. Today I noticed, in the new
Sears catalogue, that those old-fashioned, gathered curtains
Which adorned kitchen windows of the fifties
Are called "Priscillas." Cottage Priscillas.
Double- or single-draw Priscillas. Double ruffle Priscillas.

I used to be a professional chef, but I never made anything
That remotely resembles the fried chicken you get
In this neighborhood: it comes in styrofoam boxes,
With compartments of greasy macaroni salad, soggy yellow fries,
And a piece of white bread. On the lid, in relief,
"Have a Nice Day," next to an image of smiling balloons
And exclamation points scattering like bowling pins.

Life is full of surprise. Discovering the official name
Of familiar objects: one trims one's nails with pinch clippers.
The state of New York boasts good quantity
Of the following varieties of blackberry: Lawton's,
Minnewaska, and Rathburn. My next-door neighbor's dog,
The one I'd been calling "Hunter" for the last two years,

Is actually named "Putter." But back to today's topic:
Cookery. One time this guy I worked with
Told me I made the worst meat loaf he'd ever tasted *in his life*.
Another time, a drunk woman sent word to me, via a waiter,
That her eleven-year-old made a better Bolognese. Nonetheless

I persevered in my craft, so that, someday, I could afford
This box of slimy chicken, the one describing a parabola

11

Across the room, and live to write about it, on my IBM Model C.
Sun blasts the raddled limbs of a nearby birch.
Mostly, these days, we just sit around and vacuum the cats,
Play gin rummy and watch the police cars go by.
This is why I love television. Any drug that subtle
Deserves the kind of acclaim normally reserved

For a '59 Haut-Brion or (I've tasted these) a '45
Cheval Blanc. Just think of all those tuxedoed sommeliers
Stumbling from cellar to dining room, wearing
What a younger generation might see as an awesome coke spoon,
The terrific clank of it against onyx shirt studs.
This is why I love restaurants. This is one of the reasons

I like to write. It's a quiet occupation. And paper
Has its uses. You can't wrap a fish in newsreel.
It's a nice day out; it's crow season here by the bay.
A man is starting up his powerboat for the first time this year.
Clouds Vuillard never painted twirl to the west.
The dog goes off barking, into the brush.

Continental Trailways

it was in Denver
you and the girls
hitched a Corvette ride
downtown

there was a man
in a dark suit
you thought was a spy

Indianapolis' domes shone
and in Salt Lake
everything was clean

Chicago was windy
as promised

Hours after we left it
Tucumcari New Mexico
was destroyed by a tornado

St. Louis crawled
from the Mississippi
we passed through
the eye of the Arch

fire bloomed on Pittsburgh's horizon
and you saw the Supremes in Miami

but there's no place like home,
just around the corner
from the bus terminal

and this bartender
pours triple
on the third drink

which doesn't say a lot
for the first two

still, newspapers
are whirling and sliding
a quarter mile up the avenue

and a thirty-pound cat
sits
like an intelligent pear
on dirty checked linoleum

watching the front door

Flying Dublin Home

On the jet, oxygen, masks.
The pilot has a bad record.
The hostesses are addicted
to heroin. The wings
are flapping like birds' wings.

There, the World Methodist Convention
wants my hotel room.
Men gray as cement dust
melt into their beers, booze ripples
crossing the mirror like heat waves.

Four bourbons and I'm home
again, cloth pushed across
the sheen of light on wood,
and this is a place
I've never been treated badly.

Elegy for My Grandfather

When you died,
I thought of the green I'd seen, and you hadn't,
In Ireland: stone fences through train windows,
And slow, silent cobblestone streets.

I'd walk my laundry a mile,
Past cows in cropped pastures,
Then prowl the streets
Until dusk, drink dark stout

In pub corners, chat with old men and women
Who'd hang their wash in the clear air every morning,
And drink tea under a low, cumulus-heavy sky.
Later, late-night alley noises: drunks,

Headed for dawn, or somewhere else.
I like the true-stained glass of those windows,
Their arrogance in the face
Of bombs exploding up the street.

But it's too late now.
That's what I thought, this afternoon,
Headed home in the old Chevy, its wheel wells rusted
Into the shape of some ocean coast,

The clouds like babies' fists
Clenching and curling in slow motion,
In fluid blue, floating.
And as I drove down the highway's permanent ink,

I saw a sparrow hawk slant over a confusion of telephone wires,
In sunlight that turns blue eyes green,
Sunlight orange as Crenshaw melons.
Far off, over the flat thump of potato fields,

The ocean, calm and deliberate.
This isn't Ireland. You're dead.
Let's get that straight.
And the hearse I followed wasn't green,

It was gray, like the sky, or rain,
My eyes, your final perfect suit,
Your hair in the photo on the nursing home ID.
We never got to talk much.

But I'm still around,
And I remember how you taught me to draw:
Locomotives on my parents' wall.
They said you were a weak man.

I say you live, that I'm your blood,
And as I sit at this old wooden table, the evidence is everywhere:
Crocuses popping up from nowhere,
This pen clenched in my hand.

Two Shades of Gray

The lawn's alive again,
And the car at its edge
Is a new car. Along the road,
People are trying to get home,

Or leave home. The Bar & Grill lights
Are coming on, and the lumberyard's
Just shutting down. What's needed here
Is up in the air:

A swatch of pale shingles
Against pearl sky—the funeral home,
Quiet behind privet. The road
You take to get here twists,

Like a shiver up the spine
Of someone in a dark room,
And you'll pass all the hidden drive signs.
As you get closer,

The light will change:
Like the way things look through tinted glass,
Then tinted glass rolled down,
Or like the first time you put on your new glasses:

Everything, suddenly, clicking into focus.

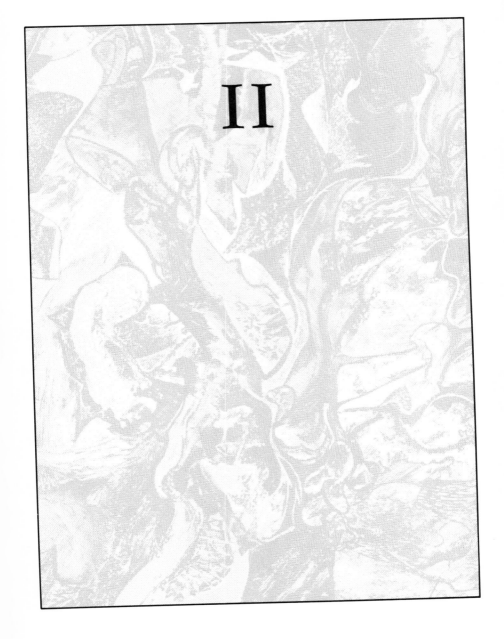

II

East Ninth Street

The Hell's Angels live one block up from here
And the *blat* of their hogs fills the morning
As I stand here on your front steps
Still wearing the dinner jacket I wore last night,
At the big-deal opening where we drank champagne

And bumped into lots of other people in tuxedoes,
Sequins, furs, and so on. And then
To the little restaurant downtown for more champagne.
Our hostess ran around, mumbling about cocaine.
Limos in a string at the curb. The moon

Looked colder than ever, and the lights
Trained on the taller buildings
Were brighter than I'd remembered. Later,
I went uptown, to smoke too much too-strong dope
And got back here at seven a.m., just as the day-old bread

Store next door opened, still in my highly polished shoes,
Bow tie starting to slide, beard appearing:
A seedy scene, really, to be all by yourself
In dinner clothes, in the morning. In a few hours,
In normal clothes, I'll walk Second Avenue, shop to shop.

Guys on the sidewalk sell things: lamps,
Styrofoam coolers, battered copies
Of *Bonjour, Tristesse.* You know, I grew up
Not far from here: I remember the old Fillmore:
The Grateful Dead, et cetera. Now I live

A hundred miles away, in what passes for exurbia.
But I keep coming back to East Ninth Street,
Or way west on 19th, or Hell's Kitchen,
Because that's where everything percolates, where
I feel most alive, most times. Maybe

I'm playing the dilettante,
But it's all out of my hands. One time,
I bought a velvet jacket from a speedfreak
On your corner. It was December. It was cold.
We had this great chat about the necessity

Of transacting business politely. We walked to the
Grocery so I could get change of a five, after
I'd tried on the jacket, out on the street.
People walked by. I had my gloves between my teeth.
"Whaddaya think," I said. "Looks good," he said.

Strange Insects

I used to live in this house with twelve cats.
After awhile, I liked them. But today, flies buzzing
        like tiny chainsaws everywhere,
I think of them as bad little machines.

Life is short, or so someone said,
And there's no time like the present, or there's no time at all.
"You know, sometimes I get this pain,"

The woman in the deli told me,
"Right through my chest, like a knife."
She continued to make tuna salad.

Another fly buzzes by.
My car sits outside quietly.
The sun is starting to get tired,

And is listing heavily toward the ocean.
A spider climbs down from the ceiling.
My friends are sitting around,

Discussing birth control.
On the window sill, a dead praying mantis.
Outside, ten acres of grass going brown.

First Day of Spring

My shoes are in their firing squad position
In the closet. My dog's dead,
But if he were here, he'd be snoring on the floor.
Accidents will happen. If you make them happen,
So much the worse. Yet

Everything goes by so quickly! The first stanza's
Already as ancient as any high school history,
And sudden absences like those leave sudden holes.
When I got cracked in the nose with a baseball bat
Playing grammar school softball,

I saw angels, Lyndon B. Johnson, and doctors
For the next three years, until my nose
Stopped bleeding and started breathing again.
You could say my nose went on a strike.
Now it veers toward Portugal

No matter where I'm headed. I'm talking
About my generation, or re-generation.
I saw my best hand-patched jeans
Hit the heap, then reappear, miraculously,
On angels walking down Main Street.

In the Red

I wish I'd seen her before.
There wasn't much to the day,
It was cool and dryish, and no one said much.
The porch was full of flowers. "Stop,"

Said the sign, and there we were,
Wondering about cocktails. She stood
Like a foxglove, like a robot,
As cool as aluminum,

Waiting for a bus. There was a fly
Buzzing around my head. It was annoying,
But nothing we hadn't expected. We had a drink.
The girl got on the bus. The bus left.

Dear black felt-tip pen, linoleum,
These are the days of our lives!
Sometime soon we'll all have lunch.
Meanwhile, the moon is crawling out

Of nothing. Lights come on.
A zip of charcoal cloud turns red.

Long Island Poets

We're all at this party,
and we all live on this island,
in one place or another.
The moon, which we're

all looking at somewhere,
is shaped like a dough-kneader,
a "D" on its side. So
what if the car's dead,

driveway blocked
and the landlady yelling
she can't sleep. That moon
slumps in its black sling

directly above the Walt Whitman
bank, and there's dirt,
tree trunks and rusting cars
everywhere! The car's

got its own mind, stalling
and clearing its throat
like nobody's business,
like the next stretch

of blue-black highway,
day-glo dashes.

It's Not the Heat It's
the Stupidity

Today's lesson: lying in the sun, for those with sensitive skin,
Is an activity to be limited, else the skin
Turns red, becomes painful, and will, after a few days,
Simply peel away. A late afternoon breeze

Rustles the hydrangea bushes, rattles the bittersweet,
Here on Happy Street. Dahlias emit rays
Of every color but red. I'm in the yard,
Waiting for carcinoma to set in.

Across the street, people are lined up like the more garish
Targets in a shooting gallery, waiting for the 4:55.
Occasionally, one dips, and I see flashing lights, hear bells,
And a man in a cheap straw hat hands me a doll. I take

It back: the bells are the train, its 300 relentless tons
Sliding by: Godzilla's fingernails on the world's largest blackboard.
I rode the local bus here this morning, because last month,
In a fit of misplaced inspiration, I drove my car

Into a tree. This morning, a boy sitting in front of me
Suddenly bolted up, pointed out a window, and yelled
"Is that who I think it is?" A five-foot twelve-year-old
Was innocently walking past a window full of espresso machines.

"He looks like he's blown out already," the boy marveled,
Sitting back down. He clutched a swim suit—black and white
Checked baggies. The last time I went swimming I lasted
About twelve minutes—all those years of smoking—

And collapsed on the sand as green flies drilled my back.
Offshore, guys in wetsuits were waterskiing,
And ninety-year-old men, fresh from quadruple bypasses,
Calmly stroked lap after lap. When I was a kid

I was an avid bicyclist, and I swam
Constantly. I had yet to acquire the taste for self-destruction
That made me want to test the resilience
Of a large, stone-like oak

With a 1976 Fleetwood Brougham with red leather upholstery
And footrests. Those days are gone. Now I spend my time
Making flamingos out of Play-doh, entering Etch-a-Sketch contests,
Throwing together *poulet aux bananes en cocotte*

For a few close friends. The kid on the bus
Reminded me of myself fifteen years ago. One time,
A guy in a tweed suit tried to pick me up
In Central Park by discussing Franz Kafka.

Some friends and I went to his place
Off Central Park West where he performed the Japanese tea ceremony
And we smoked so much hashish it took me hours
To figure out the subway route home. (I never let him touch me.)

I remember wondering why he wore tweed on such a hot day.
He gave me a copy of Dos Passos' *U.S.A.*
With his phone number on the flyleaf. I wonder
If he's still cruising Central Park benches? The blue sky

Has turned milky gray, the look of a bank of ocean fog
(The ocean's a quarter-mile away). It will rain. Tonight
I will sit with my cat in front of the television,
Watching the Boston Celtics. My heroes used to be poets;

Now they're basketball players. They are so graceful!
In their satin-shiny uniforms, the fast break uplifting.
Even guards on defense, running backwards oddly,
Are paradigms of grace. I like it when Danny Ainge, for example,

Has stolen the ball, and is running full tilt upcourt,
Launches himself into the air, knees up high, lays the ball in,
And lands, often in a heap of bodies and overturned chairs,
Behind the basket. That's entertainment. That's art.

I wish someone would ask me to endorse their product.
Robert Long, 30 word per minute typist, wears Converse All Stars.
Yes, I use Eagle Verithin pencils for the first few drafts,
Then switch to my Smith-Corona, notes William Butler Yeats,

Seen here at his desk. When I was in Ireland,
Ten years ago, there was a heat wave; it didn't rain
A single day. They were swooning in the pubs; you could have
Fried an egg on Yeats' highly polished, oddly new-looking

Gravestone. I used to like to travel. I wanted motion.
In New York City, age fourteen, I'd ride the A train
For hours, pressed up against the front window, watching
Rubies and emeralds flash in dirty tunnels,

Stutter-vision of beams bearing the number "168" or "59,"
Over and over. Sunday mornings, as sunlight rolled crosstown
From the East River, you could see me on my English racer,
Dodging cabs and Catholics, a blond blur in ripped jeans.

Once I flew to Vermont in a jet that was struck by lightning.
When we landed, I saw the pilot cleaning the windshield
With handfuls of Kleenex. It was a small jet. Since,
I've become a fan of the railroad. If I'm in

A little coffin-bunk I raise the 3 a.m. shade,
Peer onto the blue-black rails, feel the hum of
New Haven or a moonless stretch of nowhere at the heavy glass.
Here, it's ninety-four degrees,

My cat is stretched out in ragweed, the dogs
Are smiling in the shade next to their water bowl.
Boats slide in and out of the harbor, under power.
The wind has dropped, and my sneakers

Smell like burning rubber. The refrigerator is sweating.
In a former life, a fortune teller on Ninth Avenue once told me,
I played clarinet fairly well and made a killing
In oil. When I turned sixty I went nuts

And gave all my money to the Church of Latter Day Saints,
Began a cross-country walk in my one remaining suit.
That's when the crystal ball grew hazy. I paid my ten bucks,
Hit the street. Taxicabs wore halos of heat, people

Sat on stoops, fanning themselves
With the New York *Post, El Diario, La Prensa.* I bought
Some platanitos on the corner and slowly walked home,
As though underwater. They say arctic air

Is swooping in a cool arc down across Canada, that soon
We should have some relief.

Debts

Things disappear:
The glove lost in snow, pens,
Books loaned and never returned,
Virginity, your dog

Who had to be put to sleep
Because he wouldn't do it himself.
They say rules are to be broken,
But if you break one

They come knocking on the door
Right in the middle
Of a game of Parcheesi,
Or dinner, or your life.

The car's stupid grin
Lights up the driveway all night long,
And another, different dog
Twitches at the foot of the bed,

But you're still there, in the dark,
Thinking about the phone bill,
Watching the end of your cigarette:
The Incredible Glowing Skull.

Perfect Sunset

Not orange, more tangerine
Shot with LSD, the way Ivy League undergrads
Used to inject fruit with gin.

Lots of people I know
Claim that they can't "draw a straight line."
Well, I've drawn enough

To know that this pink band,
Smooth as toothpaste smeared across the horizon
Is the kind of just-right fast gesture

That you hit only once in a great while.
It's like turning on a faucet—
The floodgates opening—

And what spills out is almost secondary.
The clouds, like the insides of mattresses,
Slowly make their way

Below what we call horizon,
Beyond the borders of this page.

Hot Air

Here at this old maple table
I can hear a bell buoy clanking out in the harbor,
Past the boatyard, where dry-docked schooners and sloops
Are lined up: Wendy J. Freddy's Folly. Jimmy-Jo.
The moon's full, and there's a cold front
Resembling the meaty end of a pork chop
Blurring across the midwest.

The other night, I went out for dinner with some friends.
It wasn't a particularly auspicious occasion,
Just food. The first thing the waitress did
Was pour tea in my lap. But I refused to take this
As a bad omen, not with the way the clouds were:
Chrome smooth, fast and flat. Stars appeared
Like rhinestones, in the cold October sky.

Talking to you on the phone tonight,
I felt the static snap between us, heard the buzz and hum
Of near-disconnections, disembodied voices.
Words were lost in transmission. It was unfortunate,
As conversations go. It was unfortunate to know
That you were further away than you'd ever been,
That, stepping out into this still, clear night,
Into the shadows of the funny boats, down the creaking docks,

I'll miss you. It's not quite another world,
The imagination: just the next best thing to being there,
Thinking about phone calls, telegrams,
Wondering how distance can have heat.
And standing completely still.

In the Unfinished House

In the unfinished house, you move garbage
From one room to the next, hoping it'll disappear.
But all you get is a transformation of junk,
No matter how much you file, how much clunks into the dumpster.

These January days icicles hang like stop-action drool
From the beaks of lawn flamingos,
And rain gutters collapse, white on white with snow
As you tramp across the yard, breath frozen into thought overhead.

From the broken-down barn, you can see the whole house.
This is as good a moment to focus on as any other—
The one, let's say, where you're bending down to tie your shoes.
This is a fine time to remember

That some days things just don't feel right,
No matter what you do,
And that these sheaves of paper in shifty stacks
Are the product of a precariously ordered life,

That the house needs some attention—
Clean out the wood stoves, fix the smashed window—
That you can't let it go too long,
Let it get away from you.

III

Footnote

There is a time interval between the flash of lightning
And sound of thunder that can be measured
To determine the distance of the storm. We learn this as kids;
It's a way to locate fear, a way to control it:
Look out, dummy, there's a bus headed this way!
Screech of brakes, sighs of relief.

We saw the lightning: went outside to watch, in fact,
Heard the thunder over an opposite hill,
Noted the new, harder slant of rain in storm light.
You could see the hulls of drydocked sailboats in spidery silhouette.
Then we came back inside, and, sure enough,
Just before the racket became earsplitting, and our hair stood up,

All the lights went out. We saw it coming.
So now we're sitting here in darkness, rubbing our chins,
As Susan Hayward, waiting on Death Row, jaws with a matron in
I Want to Live. "A pair of fake earrings—
That's all I end up with," she says,
On her way to the gas chamber. This friend of mine

Advised me that pain, or at least discomfort,
Was essential to a life of learning. "Il faut souffrir . . ."
As those clever French would say. But I don't know, it's pretty
            comfortable here,
Even with no heat nor lights, small rodents scrabbling in the walls,
And there goes the TV. And one gets the feeling
That it's Evil out there, somewhere,

That's causing all these strange natural phenomena,
Even if we do know better. It's an attractive thought,
Another way to locate fear: by assuming that the whole world,
Inner or outer, is rotten to the core, anyway,
And there's no use pretending otherwise or trying to do anything

About it, about this dark room we seem to have arrived in,
With the spiders and the dead TV, as the storm begins to leave,
Lightning striking some other small community, not far from here,
And you, my döppelganger, about to be plunged into black.
It should happen to you.

What You Think You Remember

"Oh yeah," she says. "I remember those days.
It was wild. We used to dance all night,
Inhale all kinds of drugs, wonder when the sun might come up."
But that was all a long time ago.

Sometimes we get together and try on hats
But mostly we just stare out the clear blue windows
Onto the buzz of rush hour traffic
And worry about our socks falling down.

Oh baby I remember your pale blue eyes,
The way you pronounced the word "banana,"
All those scarves in your drawers.
It was like nothing I'd ever seen before.

Yeah, things have changed.
And now, all this is just a memory,
Like the music we used to listen to.
When we were kids this was what we liked:

Dirt, oil paint, sand castles, snowmen
And the cool feel of mudpies,
As though we could change anything at all.

April Again

In the restaurant,
The waitress knows you from an old place.
"I was the crazy one with the platform shoes,"
She says. You wonder if her hair was blond then,
Or red. Or in the yard, distant buzz saws droning,
Where the light is brighter
Than all of the world's restaurants.

You remember a barbecue with your parents
That lasted through evening: citronella burning,
Fog lowering over the bay. Though you were young,
You suddenly knew what this meant.
And then the stars appearing.

This is a blue we can't hold in our hands,
Though Lord knows we try, the sky reflected
In workshirts and jeans. A boat sits peeling
On its trailer, and a little dog starts to yap.
Falling into spring again, you can spot
Men working on the roads,
The same hitchhiker going in the opposite direction.

What's So Funny 'Bout Peace, Love
and Understanding

At the party she said
"You only want what you can't have,"
As you smashed into a locked door.
Give up. The telephone's exploding
With all the wrong numbers, and,
Yes, the blank wall's fascinating,
So who needs sleep?

Here's someone breathing
Appropriate exhortations in your ear,
Here's someone else
With a twelve-in-one knife,
Here's the guy in the deli
Calling you "sir"
As he wraps the roast beef.

I remember adolescence.
It went by in a blur of hallucinogens,
Peace signs, and speechlessness: days,
Hot beach, then the beach at night:
That perfect sleep sound,
And the stars,
Like push pins in really lovely material.

Heightened Boredom

We stole some tulips from a friend's garden
Last night, because someone was coming with a camera,
And we wanted the place to look nice.
Then some people arrived, so we stood on the lawn
Listening to jets going by. What's wrong
With this picture?

I grew up in the city, but the country
Seems more like the city to me now.
Trees rustling, machinery dredging the harbor,
Clouds forming the profile of each of the 40 odd
Presidents of the United States, in correct order.
Such process! Things so shifty

They acquire a permanence.
An enthusiastic Malamute comes bounding out of a bush,
And I have a minor heart attack.
Earlier, I washed my car with a hose,
Then sat staring, thinking of you.
The mailman's coming down the road now

In his red white and blue Jeep. Here he is.

Somewhere on the Coast of Maine

I think I like it here, I mean I think
There's something attractive about the ocean's way
Of insinuating itself into anyone's life,
As if salt air could solve anything, as if
That watery presence insured a special kind of luck,

Some new variety of insurance:
Like walking out onto the street and knowing
That a bus will come by to take you up- or down-
Or cross-town. All you need is ninety cents
And a half-decent haircut. I like

The way the sun comes down, here:
It's kind of sweet, and calm: orange
And aquamarine over all that field, that green stretch
Of quiet, despite everything. Here's what I'm talking about:
The way you dragged me all over the island

Your parents own, that curious enthusiasm;
Let's keep this on hold, this anyone
Who's close to you. But I don't want to veer
Away from things. Listen,
I love Maine as much as the next guy,

Maybe more so. There's nothing like mussels
Fresh-scrubbed, cooked in a little white wine, and there's nothing
Like the 7 a.m. view from my window, of the sun
Shining bravely over New England, and everyone:
Your parents, your sister and two nephews,

Sitting downstairs, scrambling eggs, brewing coffee,
Thinking only of breakfast, or extensions of breakfast:
Say, that time I made a complicated pasta
Which served as lunch, the next day. I like pasta.
I *love* pasta. Don't you? Lately, I've become fond

Of movies starring Rod Taylor, movies
From the late sixties: limousines, diplomats from Australia.
But back to Maine: It was swell.
I'm glad we went. Someday
I'll drop you a postcard describing exactly how swell it was,

But I don't think you're ready for it, quite yet.
Such indecision—where, when, why—
Leads to a kind of illumination; by crossing off
Obvious possibilities on the List of What One Does,
One can't help but be steered, like a drunken tourist,

In the direction of novelty. The snow that came
When we wanted it to snow. Encounters
With hostile men in gun shops: I almost bought it,
That beautiful 30.06 we ran into. Those guys
Were real nice; they nearly blew off our heads

For breathing, but what the heck. It comes
With the territory. I had this friend who wrote mysteries
For a living, but he died. The last thing he told me
Was to keep things "light." I've never
Been able to understand exactly what he meant by that—

I mean, I actually think about these things—

But such advice seems appropriate,
Here in Friendship, Maine, where we had
Two or three games of pool (I lost)
And a few beers, where we cruised the wet highway
Endlessly: the slow slope of hills,

The mystery of landscape turning gray-blue at dusk,
Where I loved you, for better or for worse,
Ex post facto, purely confidential,
In the little white Honda, wishing
We were somewhere else.

Dreaming

It's 3 a.m., and I'm thinking
About how, lately, I've been on the phone too much,
How many bad movies I've seen.
Bad movies: a whole new sphere of influence.
Let's talk about sentimentality,
How one can become overly fond of poached eggs,
Or slurry black and white images:
Newsprint or video. Distorted memories.
How I loved you. How I learned Pakistani.

For example: watch any late-night Western,
Note the bullet holes, stampedes,
Flaming pots of java. This was years ago.
Violins creep in. It's all too obvious.
You know, I get the paper, I get the news,
But there's something ineluctable
You want. Let's talk. This is exurbia, 1983,
And all your friends are married, or dead,
Or worse. But you're exaggerating, as usual.

As usual, you're wearing just one
Of your fifty-seven shirts. You like shirts.
I like you. You don't seem to understand.
Sometimes I think I'll just climb in my silver car
With a sheet of purple blotter
And about a pound of Bolivian rock.
I'll just sit there for a few months, or more.
Remember, it takes years
For certain dull spells to wear off.

And this one will. It'll be like
One of those moments in Hollywood musicals
Where day-to-day events
Erupt into furious tap dancing, applause
Like an ice storm, lots of teeth.
All that. Spinning headlines. Someday,
We'll know what they say.
Or so we'd like to think.

Old Story

Climbing into bed, you hear a car start:
It sounds like a machine gun in a garbage can.
A light blinks off, and the ceiling's faint blue glow,
Like the way your teeth looked in blacklight
In your friend's cellar, at sixteen, ceases.

Say a woman walked up to you in a deli and said
"You look like someone who pays taxes."
Could you figure it? Maybe you look responsible
Staring at smoked salmon, chicken salad, tins of snuff.
Maybe not. Maybe you're innocently waiting for the mailman

And you get arrested for sneezing.
Maybe you go home with someone
And they beat you to death with a box of Cheerios.
How about the old Chance Meeting
With Unrequited Love: In Person: One Night Only:

The snappy chatter, the stuttering, like a TV commercial
For anxiety and ecstasy, all smashed up in one.
Vodka doesn't help. It gets late. You both go home.
Why can't this get any simpler? I mean "this"
In a vague fashion, you know the gesture:

Hands fanning out in the general direction
Of lamps, telephones, Scrabble, dying flamingos,
The late Beethoven quartets, rock and roll,
Chocolate ice cream and sex. You know the rest.
Sometimes all you want is a little sleep,

Especially the dream about a mysterious place
Where elevators go sideways, and you're always flying
Seven feet above the ground, heading somewhere else.

Saying One Thing

Today, the angels are all writing postcards,
Or talking on the telephone.
Meanwhile, in Nowheresville,
A rabbit is running into a bush. This, I tell my friend,
Means good luck. The next day,
The sun is out, the fix is in,

And we're ready to throw in the towel.
Anytime now, our number might come up,
And the telephone will finally stop ringing:
Don't call before three,
Knock four times,
Show me the way to go home,

Back and forth and back again,
Like some idiot boomerang.
"Kerpow" and "schlock" are our favorite words,
Lately, and are about what things are amounting to.
Still, the stories of airplane disasters
And overnight flings in far-off cities have a kind of allure,

Like metallic paint, or something expensive
You want but can't have.
O toothpaste commercials, common house fly,
Fall is in the air again. On this spaceship
The code word is "blonde," or "good dog."
Night begins to fall, the atmosphere is electric.

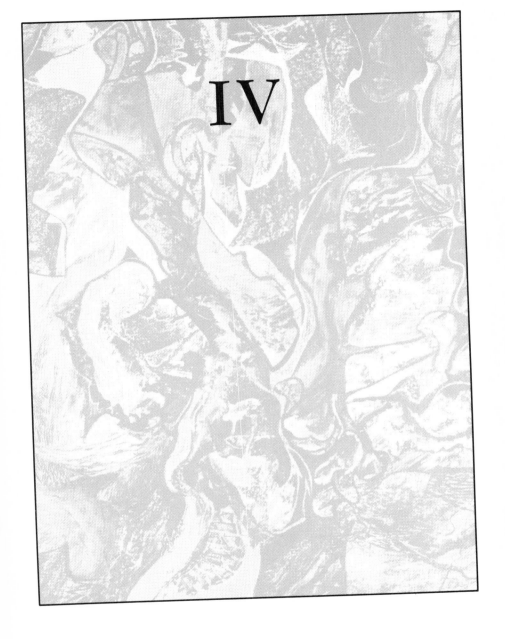

What It Is

Fondly we count the clouds
As they pass like boxcars. Out on the lawn,
Someone is reading a history
Of French court life: "Marie Antoinette
Bid the servant enter, and, disapproving
Of his mien, sent him out again."

Inside, someone's grinding coffee beans.
A barn swallow flies past the single sunflower,
The clipped hedge, an insect-like tractor,
And, finally, into coruscations flashing like dimes
On the ocean: too flashy for me, but, behind sunglasses,
Gray, and almost austere: tasteful.

I've got a cold, my car's out of gas,
And I can't shake this feeling of helplessness:
The sun glides by on its oiled track.
We watched our friends heading out to have a bad time;
We had nothing to say to each other.
But this is a kind of ecstasy:

Power lines looping to the roof,
Shadow of a bird crossing the lawn.
For awhile I thought I'd die young.
This is for you,
Voice from the sky confused with clouds and slogans,
Old plaid shirt like a strange flag,

Birds who never sleep.
Rabbit in the headlights,
Old sneakers filled with sand, beware:
The time is ripe.
Our days are numbered.

Leaving Vermont

On the train, you see
A field full of decoys,
Wooden silhouettes,
Half-bent to peck at snow;

Leaves and needles;
Light on wood; bubbles
Rising through a bottleneck
Like smoke rings.

That state meant nothing.
You stood like a doll
At the edge of everything,
Watching it dance away.

A simple notebook vibrates
On the pull-down bed.
In the sky, cold, white rock.
The train's got the shakes

Tonight. Cars sleep in drifts
By the tracks. These twisted
Characters, milestones
On the highway of the page.

Interior Decoration

Today, my lawn mower stared
Through the sliding glass doors
Like a small, automated animal.
Birds, too, fly through these doors;

They remind me of wind-up toys.
When I was a kid,
They dressed me in blazers and black socks.
Now, I'm grown up

And I'm fond of sailboats and emphysema.
The lobsters are doing the hula down by the docks.
A barge groans. Listen:
The little blue dots on the horizon of your eyes

Remind me of blue spruce,
Or a throw-away razor, the kind
You buy on the run.
Outside, a bird makes a noise like a berserk computer,

And the sun heads for the rotting bulkhead.
I don't like this kind of waiting:
The wildlife is patient, like concrete.
Nothing changes. "This room needs flowers."

December

It's the middle of December,
And I'm trying to sleep in a strange bed.
Downstairs, the furnace clicks on,
And plaster starts to rumble.
Upstairs, a knee knocks the wall.

I'm thinking of you,
And you don't deserve it.
Imagine the particular smash of a brick
Thrown through plate glass,
Or a boot grinding anything to pulp;

That's how I'm thinking of you.
But never mind; if anything like that
Happened, I'd be the first one there,
With all sorts of lifesaving devices.
Too bad.

Anyhow, sucker, maybe you'll be walking
Down the street someday,
And everything will change:
Cracks in cement will seem abysmal,
Faces nasty maps of ill-led lives,

Even the trees will be threatening,
As in bad movies,
And your life will make a U-turn for the worst.
I wish this on you, I wish you
Forced to think harder than you've ever had to,

And then maybe you'll realize
That soon you'll be as dead as anything.
The world will continue for billions of years
Without your dim light,
Which grows dimmer by the minute,

The more I let myself think of you,
Wasting my own short time.

Time and Its Double

St. Lucy is the patron saint of eyes. A friend told me
She was haunted, in childhood, by a statue, in Corona, Queens,
Of Lucy holding a dish full of eyeballs. This is part of the dream
I had last night, brought on by a TV commercial:

Me, in a chaise, basking on the sands
Of St. Bart's, or one of those other chichi isles
Named for men who were shot full of arrows, or stoned by the
    populace,
Or each other, or wandered around mumbling to themselves.

As we drive off into the slate early evening, we think of Lucy,
Send her a prayer. You know, every month around this time
I get a package from the Dessert-of-the-Month Club, to which I've
    belonged
For going on three years. One time,

L'île flottante came to my door, and Carol Ann had to take a Valium.
Carol Ann wore tanktops and cutoffs and slept a lot. Awake,
She worked on her dissection of Keats, read Bachelard
Over and over, went to writing seminars, while I fed the cats,

Worked in the garden. One day, it was over.
"No man hath seen God at any time," Scripture insists,
And that includes all our acid trips and eerie feelings
Atop Irish hills at the feet of which our ancestors were buried.

On the road tonight, we note animal corpses, cool crescents
Of moon reflected in sliding glass doors, consider the Unknown
    Sex Lives
Of the saints, dead Popes, the Jesuits who taught me algebra.
How did sex enter their formulae? Is there a doctoral thesis in here,

Somewhere? Late at night we compare notes: What's America's
Favorite hobby? Who's buried in Grant's Tomb? The cats
Gallop across the room, make worried, bird-like trills,
Collapse on their sides and chew table legs. Outside,

A man walks by with a dachshund wearing an argyle sweater.
This is the universe I was afraid I really had landed in,
When I was nine, and, much as I try to disguise it, I'm still
That reserved blond kid you see in grade school photos,

The kind with ether-like, milky blue backgrounds, though they
    were taken
At the gate to Hell, in this case, the cafeteria. Ladies and
    gentlemen,
There's something to be said for a regular program each day:
In bed by eleven, up by seven. People like you help people like me

Go on, on into the dusk, where kidney beans are being cooked to
    mush,
To be spooned into taco shells. It all reminds me
Of Kansas City, where I was brought once, but that's another story.

Found and Lost

Let's tell the story of the man
Who worked in a factory, making chocolate cigarettes,
Who ran over a squirrel on his way to work
One morning: it belched a cloud of CO_2,

Vanished in the mirror. The man
Mourned. He began collecting photographs
Of squirrels. The walls of his home
Bore them: soon, he became

A recognized authority on the squirrel,
Its anatomy, its habits, its relationship
To other rodents. People became tired
Of his singular devotion, began

Posting bills on walls all over town,
Posters reading "Down With Squirrels," and
"Turn on the TV so I can see if I'm alive."
The man moved to North Dakota,

Where he died. Let's call him John.
He wasn't much fun. Sometimes I can almost feel
How he must have felt, that burden
Of guilt, that siege of unpopularity.

Distance has its disadvantages. You're
In Paris, trying on shoes, and I'm wondering
If it's really snowing out or if it's just
Blowing off the trees. The distance

From me to you a slow motion stretch
Of ocean air, nearly palpable, heavy,
Heavier by the second. It's late fall,
And it's too late to start over.

Alert

Wake up. The situation here is getting worse, and,
No, I'm not over anything. What I'm onto
Is the middle-of-the-night starts, where you stop sleeping
And start staring at blank corners.
You want to clean the whole house immediately.
You make the bed just to convince yourself
That life is something you can organize,
That there's something palpable about it,

That if you get everything externalized—
Socks in order, jeans neatly stacked,
The lawn raked, the car inspected—
Everything will fall into place. It doesn't.
One second you're dreaming conversations
With various pets, old friends, lovers, and then—bingo—
You're up in bed, wondering who and why you are.

Goodbye

It's a hot day, and I'm sweating
Out the fact that you're gone for good,
That you never loved me
Like I loved you, as the sky
Turns the color of milk: dense, humid,
Halyards clanking a little in the smallest breeze.

All my life I've lived near water:
Rivers around Manhattan, the ocean, bays, and now,
This soggy marina, slathered with sunlight.
Across the uncut lawn,
Through a line of baby spruce,
I can hear the water's slap on fiberglass, wood.

Further off, two egrets fold into marsh grass.
I'm glad you're gone. It gets me
Into my work and out of my mind. I wish
You luck. Out of luck and into myself,
I want to want you somewhere else,
I'd like to not like you as I do.

Slabs of gray cloud unfold:
Air as still as the moment after a yawn.
Boats are quiet: tethered, docked.
Birds start going bananas. Stop it:
It's enough, being here at all, in this same room,
Tide going out, sun going down.

What Happens

"Let's say that grief has insisted that you carry
its luggage. That you have no choice."
—MEKEEL McBRIDE

Let's say that what I miss
Is the sound of your car door whining open,
Then slamming lightly, and the two minute delay
While you walked up the little hill,
Carrying folders and pens, or a soccer ball, or, once,
A tackle box with a snapping turtle shut inside.
You found him on the road. We called him Marcel.
He lay for weeks on the bottom of his tank,
And never got used to it, though he ate raw meat
Thoughtfully, one half-inch chunk at a time.
He was a meditative creature; he stared into the corners
Of his little home for whole days. He wasn't impressed
When we'd stare back, or talk to him, or play music.

But enough of strange pets. It's not enough,
Remembering events as though they held such significance—
Such nearly physical import—that they could matter.
What's the use. What's the right way to say goodbye?
Maybe it means throwing out words like these:
Old blue sweatshirt. One bottle rubbing alcohol.
A quart jar reading WATER. Letters.
It's impulse that rules us, the impulse that causes
Certain days to be memorable, this possibility:
Anything can happen, and will. It's the feeling
That anytime now, this hot July sun will fade
Behind stratocirrus, that sheets of rain will lacquer
These windows. Here today, and gone tomorrow,
All you've got coming is the moment.

When we let the snapping turtle go,
He plonked like a stone dropped casually into the pond.
As the rings on the water grew thoughtfully distant,
Highway noise drifted in. I remember touching you
Lightly, on the shoulder. A kid dropped his toy boat,

On the opposite shore. We headed back to the car,
Just after the little bubbles glugged to the surface.
I shut my door. The clouds were passing above
In confident gangs, and we drove the twist of roads home,
The place by the water, the home you'd leave in a matter of days,
Our lives as confused and clear as hieroglyphics. This moment:
Leaves turning silver. A backache that comes and goes.

Chelsea

I'm comfortable here, on 50 mg. of Librium,
Two hundred bucks in my pocket
And a new job just a week away.
I can walk the streets in a calm haze,
My blood pressure down to where I'm almost human,
Make countless pay-phone calls from street corners:
Buzzing, they go by in near-neon trails,
People, people like me, headed for black bean soup,
For screams in alleyways, for the homey click
Of the front door's closing, heading home
Past all those faces you know you've seen before:
Like a rear-screen projection in an old movie,
The actors pacing a treadmill or pretending to steer,
And the same '56 Dodge weaving in the background.

It's like walking into a room
And suddenly realizing you've had sex with everyone there
At least once, watching your friends' lives
Tangling as you all grow somewhat older,
Somehow more resolute. Bookshelves grow, too,
And you notice your handwriting becoming more matter-of-fact.
It's as if all that comic smartness we glided through in youth
Were somehow desperate. And now we come to terms
With the sidewalk's coruscating glamour,
The rows of dull but neat garbage cans,
Each with its own painted number,
The poodles and patrol cars, the moon rising high,
Like aspirin, over Eighth Avenue.

I get some cigarettes on a corner,
Catch my reflection in the glass. I'm neatly tranquilized,
And strangely happy just to walk out near the traffic,
Consider the asphalt intersections where kids lean on lamp posts
              and fire alarms,

Where a man is shutting the iron gate on his ochre divans,
Where the beautiful taxis whizz and honk,
Clanking over sewer covers and smashing beer cans.
And windows light, one by one, like comic strip inspirations,
And me, here, on your street corner,
In my second-favorite neighborhood in the world,
My index finger in the hole marked "9,"
Ready for anything, finally, and finally ready.

Dedications

Water: for Heather McHugh
Montauk Point: in memory of Doris Planz
Thruway: for Mary Karr
Flying Dublin Home: for Richard Hugo
East Ninth Street: for Maria Maraventano
First Day of Spring: for Lisa Britz
In the Red: for Josh Dayton
Long Island Poets: for Graham Everett
In the Unfinished House: for Allen Planz
Footnote: for Mary Karr
Old Story: for Ali Cole
Saying One Thing: for Daisy Jacobs
What It Is: for Krys Powell
Chelsea: for Marion Lowe

ROBERT LONG was born in New York City, in 1954. He is the author of *The Sonnets* (Illuminati, 1988) and two chapbooks, *Getting Out of Town* (1978) and *What It Is* (1981), both from Street Press, as well as the editor of *Long Island Poets* (The Permanent Press, 1986), a compilation of the works of twenty-seven poets associated with the Eastern End of Long Island. Mr. Long was awarded the Yeats Fellowship of Long Island University while an undergraduate there, which sent him to Ireland, and was also awarded the 1986 Faculty Poetry Prize of Long Island University. He received his M.F.A. in Writing from Vermont College in 1984. Currently, he is Adjunct Associate Professor of English at LIU/Southampton, and also works as an art critic. He lives in East Hampton.

Sandcastle Seahorses, a children's story by Nikia Leopold
Life in the Middle of the Century, two novellas by John Dranow
The Halo of Desire, poetry by Mark Irwin
The Eye That Desires To Look Upward, poetry by Steven Cramer
The Four Wheel Drive Quartet, a fiction by Robert Day
New World Architecture, poetry by Matthew Graham
The Maze, poetry by Mick Fedullo
Keeping Still, Mountain, poetry by John Engman
On My Being Dead and Other Stories, by L. W. Michaelson
The Intelligent Traveler's Guide to Chiribosco, a novella
    by Jonathan Penner